A Fre

I want to say Thank You for buying my book so I put together a free gift for you!

"The Quinoa Desserts Recipe Book"

This gift is the perfect complement to this book so if you want it sent to you just visit:

www.GoodLivingPublishing.com/Quinoa

Contents

Introduction

Quinoa is becoming increasingly popular yet it still remains an unknown food to most people. It has lurked in the corners of the dietary world for years and only now is it beginning to fully reveal itself.

This means that many people have skipped over this delicious gluten free, protein packed grain without knowing just how amazing it is, and why they need it in their life.

Incredibly high in protein, packed with vitamins and full of fibre quinoa is truly a super-food.

Not only is it a super-food but it's also incredibly versatile and can be used in everything from soups to desserts.

In this book I am going to cover a whole host of recipes that will get you more quinoa in your diet. The book is split into breakfast, lunch and dinner recipes but you don't need to adhere to this structure. Nearly all the lunch recipes are suitable for dinner and vice-versa.

Every recipe is absolutely bursting with flavour, simple to make and best of all... can be stored and eaten later. This is one of the most incredible things about quinoa – you can cook a recipe in advance and it will still taste amazing a few days later. Quinoa can be eaten hot or cold so it means that your leftover food is perfect for taking to work the next day.

As quinoa is perfect for gluten free and vegetarian diets the vast majority of the recipes in this book are vegetarian and gluten-free. Any recipe that isn't compliant with these diets has been clearly specified.

If you're new to quinoa I also included a chapter all about the benefits eating it delivers. If you've ever wondered what makes quinoa a super-food... go check out that section.

So, grab those pots and pans because it's time to whip up some healthy, delicious and nutritious quinoa meals that will leave you wondering where this super-food has been all your life.

Why Should I Eat Quinoa?

Well, the short answer is… it's a super-food. To add to that it's arguably the best super-food available.

Although the short answer is delightfully sweet, I want to also give you a longer explanation so I can highlight just how amazing quinoa is.

So, what makes quinoa so amazing?

Well, it is high in protein, full of vitamins, gluten free, contains all 9 amino acids and packs almost twice the fibre of other grains.

This means that eating quinoa will help you lose weight, feel healthier, improve your energy levels, build muscle, reduce high blood pressure and lower your cholesterol.

Oh, and it will also save you money due to its low cost. I should also mention that you will almost never waste quinoa as it is so versatile and 'keeps' for a very long time.

I mentioned that quinoa is packed with vitamins. If you were wondering which vitamins, here is quick list for you: Iron, Calcium, Potassium, Vitamin E, Riboflavin, Magnesium, Linolenic Acid and Folic Acid.

As quinoa is one of the most protein rich foods available eating it will massively help you lose weight. Protein keeps you feeling fuller longer and diets high in protein are an excellent way to shed those unwanted pounds. Combine this with its high fibre content and you have a weight-loss super-food.

I could wax on about in detail about all the amazing benefits quinoa delivers but I have a feeling you're itching to get onto the recipes. To that note I will close this by saying…

You should be eating quinoa because it will improve your health. It will make you look better, feel better and given its 'healthy heart' properties it may very well make you live longer.

So dive into the recipes and check out just how versatile this delicious super-food is.

Breakfast Recipes

Quinoa Scrambled Eggs

Makes 1-2 Servings.

Ingredients

½ cup quinoa, cooked

2 large eggs

½ avocado, scooped out of the skin and sliced

½ cup salsa

1 tbsp olive oil

Sea salt and black pepper, to taste

Directions

Place a small pan over a medium-low heat and add the olive oil.

Crack the eggs into a bowl, sprinkle in black pepper and salt. Whisk well.

Add the eggs to the pan and use a spatula to keep them moving.

Once the eggs are cooked and well scrambled (around 3-4 minutes) turn off the heat.

Add the avocado and salsa, fold them into the eggs.

Let the latent heat from the pan heat the salsa and avocado.

Speedy Breakfast Bowl

Makes 1-2 Servings.

Ingredients

½ cup quinoa, cooked

¼ cup milk

Honey, to taste

1 banana, chopped

5 strawberries, halved

Handful of chopped almonds

Directions

Add the cooked quinoa to a bowl and then add the milk. Mix well.

Add the banana, strawberries and almonds. Gently mix.

Drizzle honey over everything.

Breakfast Muffin

Makes 6-8 Muffins.

Not suitable for Gluten Free Diet.

Ingredients

1 & ¾ cups wholemeal flour

½ cup quinoa, cooked

1 & ½ tsp cinnamon

1 large egg

½ cup sugar

½ cup honey

2 tsp baking powder

½ tsp baking soda

½ cup vegetable oil

The juice and zest of 2 oranges

1 cup buttermilk

Directions

Preheat your oven to 375F.

In a large mixing bowl combine the wholemeal flour, quinoa, cinnamon, sugar, baking soda and baking powder. Whisk to mix together and set aside.

In another bowl add the egg, buttermilk, honey, oil and orange zest/juice. Whisk to mix well.

Pour this into the flour mixture and mix until well combined.

Line a muffin tray/tin with liners. Pour or spoon the mixture into the liners leaving a small space at the top.

Add a sprinkle more of quinoa over the top of everything and then put in the oven.

Bake for 20 minutes, the top should be golden brown.

Scrumptious Omelette

Makes 1-2 Servings.

Ingredients

3 large eggs

¼ onion, thinly sliced

¼ cup sun-dried tomatoes, chopped

1 clove of garlic, minced

¼ tsp red pepper or chilli flakes

1 handful spinach, washed

½ cup quinoa, cooked

¼ cup goats cheese, crumbled

Black pepper and salt, to taste

2 tbsp olive oil

Directions

Place a pan over a medium heat and add 1 tbsp olive oil.

Add the eggs to a bowl, beat and set aside.

Once the pan begins to heat add the onions and garlic. Cook until the onions become translucent, about 4-5 minutes.

Add the tomatoes, chilli flakes and spinach.

Mix well and cook until the spinach is wilted. Sprinkle with salt and pepper. Then transfer this mixture to a separate bowl.

Add the goats cheese to the mixture, fold and then leave to stand.

Add the remaining 1 tbsp of oil to the pan and then add the eggs.

As the eggs cook remember to run your spatula around the rim to prevent sticking.

After 4-5 minutes spoon your tomato, spinach and goats cheese mixture onto one half of the omelette.

Carefully fold the other half of the omelette over the top. Continue to cook for 2 minutes.

Gluten Free Breakfast Cake

1 Cake Will Yield 8-10 Servings.

Ingredients

⅔ cup almond meal

⅔ cup sorghum flour

½ cup quinoa flakes, not whole quinoa

¼ cup tapioca starch

2 tsp baking powder

½ tsp baking soda

¾ teaspoon xanthan gum

1 tsp sea salt

1 tsp cinnamon

½ tsp ginger, ground

¼ tsp nutmeg, ground

½ cup maple syrup

¼ cup coconut oil, melted

3 large eggs, beaten

2 tbsp coconut milk

2 tsp bourbon vanilla

1 tsp almond extract

1 packed cup zucchini, shredded or finely chopped

Directions

Line a cake pan or loaf tray with parchment paper.

Preheat your over to 350F.

Add the almond meal, flour, tapioca, baking powder, gum, quinoa, salt, cinnamon, ginger and nutmeg to a large mixing bowl. Whisk everything together.

Once mixed add the maple syrup, coconut oil, eggs and the coconut milk. Mix everything together and if the batter is too thick add 1 tbsp more coconut milk.

Pour in the vanilla and almond extract to the mixture, beat until smooth.

Add the zucchini and mix in with your hands.

Spoon or pour the mixture into the cake pan and then sprinkle the top with water.

Bake for 30 minutes in your oven. The top should be golden and when you stab through the cake with a tooth pick it should emerge clean.

Let cool, ideally on a wire rack.

Family Pancakes

Makes 4 Servings.

Not Suitable for Gluten Free Diet.

Ingredients

1 cup quinoa, cooked

¾ cup all-purpose flour

2 tsp baking powder

½ tsp sea salt

1 large egg

1 large egg white

1 tbsp unsalted butter, melted

2 tbsp unsalted butter (for greasing pan)

¼ cup milk

2 tbsp maple syrup

Directions

Whisk the quinoa, flour, baking powder and salt together in a medium bowl.

In a different bowl whisk the egg, egg white, melted butter, milk and syrup. The mixture should be smooth.

Add the two mixtures together and whisk until they are combined.

Place a pan over a medium-high heat and grease with butter.

Add the pancake mixture by spooning it out and letting it "drop" into the pan. Cook for around 2 minutes, or until bubbles start to show on top.

Flip and cook for a further 2-3 minutes. Wipe the pan and repeat the process.

Whilst cooking the other pancakes keep the cooked ones warm in the oven.

Serve with more maple syrup and fresh fruit if desired.

Quinoa Breakfast Burrito

Makes 2 Servings.

Not Suitable for Gluten Free & Vegetarian Diet

Ingredients

½ cup quinoa, cooked

½ cup salsa

1" of chorizo sausage, chopped

1 red bell pepper, chopped

½ onion, finely chopped

½ tsp garlic, minced

1 tbsp olive oil

Hot sauce, to taste

¼ cup grated cheese

1 or 2 whole wheat tortilla wraps

Directions

Place a pan over a medium heat and add the olive oil.

Once the oil is heated add the onions. Cook for 2 minutes.

Add the pepper and garlic. Cook for a further 5 minutes or until peppers are soft.

Throw in the chorizo and cook for 2 minutes.

Add the cooked quinoa and salsa, cook until it is heated through. Ensuring everything is well mixed.

Turn off the heat and add the grated cheese. Let the cheese melt, toss the mixture once or twice.

Spoon onto the wraps and fold up.

Stuffed Pears

Makes 1-2 Servings.

Ingredients

1 pear, halved with a hole scooped out each middle

½ cup quinoa, cooked

½ cup dried fruit and nut mix

2 tbsp honey

¼ cup natural yoghurt

Directions

Add the quinoa, fruit & nut mix and the honey to a mixing bowl. Mix well and ensure everything is well coated in honey.

Scoop mixture into the pear holes.

Drizzle the yoghurt over everything.

If you want to add more honey and fruit to the top of this before serving then go ahead.

Apple & Cinnamon Bites

Makes 3-4 Servings.

Ingredients

1 cup quinoa, cooked

1 cup quick cook oatmeal (if gluten free ensure you buy gluten free oats)

½ tsp cinnamon

½ tsp nutmeg

3 tbsp brown sugar

1 tbsp granulated sugar

1 tbsp maple syrup

1 cup chopped apple

2 eggs, beaten

Directions

Preheat your oven to 350F.

Add the quinoa and oatmeal to a large mixing bowl and mix together.

In a different bowl add the cinnamon, nutmeg and both sugars. Mix this well and then add to the quinoa/oatmeal mixture. Mix well.

Now add the eggs, maple syrup and chopped apple. Mix well.

Take a muffin pan (ideally a mini-muffin pan) and coat well with oil spray.

Spoon the mixture into each muffin slot and then bake for 20 minutes.

Makes 1 Serving.

Ingredients

1 cup Greek yogurt

½ cup quinoa, cooked

½ tsp vanilla extract

½ tsp ground cinnamon

1 banana, chopped

1 tbsp peanut butter

¼ cup dried fruit and nut mix

Directions

In a whisky glass (rocks glass) layer the parfait in the following way:

½ cup of Greek yogurt

Layer of banana slices

½ cup of quinoa mixed with the vanilla and cinnamon

Layer of banana slices

½ cup of Greek yogurt

Sprinkle the top with fruit and nut mix. Add a dollop of peanut butter to finish it all off.

Lunch Recipes

Edamame Quinoa Salad

Makes 2-3 Servings.

Ingredients

1 cup quinoa, uncooked

2 cups vegetable broth

2 cups frozen shelled edamame, thawed

1 tbsp freshly grated lemon zest

2 tbsp freshly squeezed lemon juice

2 tbsp olive oil

2 tsp dried tarragon

½ tsp sea salt

½ cup roasted red peppers from a jar, chopped

¼ cup chopped walnuts

Directions

Place a pan over a medium heat and add the quinoa. Dry toast the quinoa for about 5 minutes, be sure to keep it moving.

Add the quinoa to a sieve and rinse. Set aside

Add the broth to the pan and bring to a boil over a medium heat. Pour the quinoa back into the pan and return to the boil.

Reduce the heat, cover and let simmer for 6-8 minutes. Remove the lid and add the edamame, don't stir.

Place the lid back on the pan and cook until both the edamame and quinoa are tender. Should take around 8-10 minutes for all the broth to be absorbed.

In a large bowl whisk together the zest, lemon juice, oil, tarragon and salt.

Add the chopped peppers and quinoa to the bowl and toss together.

Top with chopped walnuts before serving.

Greek Salad

Makes 3-4 servings.

Ingredients

1 & ½ cup quinoa, uncooked

2 cups water

Sea salt, to taste

1 cup chopped cucumber

½ cup cherry tomatoes, diced

¼ cup olives, chopped

½ red onion, chopped

2 green onions, chopped

Juice from 1 lemon

3 tbsp olive oil

2 tbsp white wine vinegar

2 cloves of garlic, minced

½ cup feta cheese

Directions

Add the water to a pot along with the quinoa and bring to the boil over a medium-high heat.

Reduce the heat to medium-low and let simmer (covered) for 15-18 minutes. Take off the heat.

In a large bowl mix together the cucumber, tomatoes, olives and onions. Set aside

To make the dressing whisk the lemon juice, olive oil, vinegar, garlic, the salt and the pepper.

Mix together the quinoa and vegetables. Drizzle the dressing over everything.

Makes 2 Servings.

Ingredients

1 cup quinoa, cooked

½ cup sliced almonds

¼ cup toasted sunflower seeds

½ cup dried cranberries

2 cups spinach, torn

For the dressing

4 tbsp apple cider vinegar

4 tbsp olive oil

1 tsp honey

Salt and pepper to taste

Directions

Firstly make the dressing by adding the ingredients to a bowl and mixing well. Set aside

In a large bowl mix all the remaining ingredients together.

Drizzle the dressing over and toss well. Place in the refrigerator for an hour to allow the quinoa to absorb the flavours of the dressing.

Black Bean Mix

This recipe will make 3-4 servings.

Ingredients

¼ tsp olive oil

½ onion, finely chopped

1 clove of garlic, minced

½ cup quinoa, uncooked

⅓ cup vegetable broth

Sprinkle of ground cumin

Sprinkle of cayenne pepper

Salt and pepper to taste

¼ cup of frozen corn kernels

½ cup of black beans

2 tbsp chopped cilantro

Direction

Place a small pan over a medium heat and add the oil. When the oil is heated add the onion and garlic. Cook for 4-5 minutes or until the onion is translucent.

Add the quinoa to the pan and mix well with the onion and garlic. Add the vegetable broth, cumin, cayenne, salt and pepper. Bring to the boil before covering and reducing the heat to a simmer.

Let simmer for 20 minutes before removing the cover and adding the frozen corn kernels. Mix well and continue to let simmer for a further 5 minutes.

Add the black beans and cilantro. Mix together. Cook for a further 1-2 minutes.

Makes 2-3 Servings.

Ingredients

2 tbsp olive oil

1 onion, finely chopped

2 cloves of garlic, minced

1 cup quinoa, uncooked

2 cups chicken or vegetable broth

1 tbsp curry powder, and more to taste

1 tbsp Ancho Chilli powder

Salt and pepper, to taste

Directions

Place a pan over a medium heat, add the oil and heat it. Once heated add the onion and garlic. Cook for 5 minutes or until the onion is translucent.

Pour the cup of quinoa in and mix well. Allow to roast in the oil but be sure to stir continually to prevent it sticking to the pan.

After 3-4 minutes add the broth and bring to a boil.

Reduce the heat, add the curry and chilli powder, and mix the seasoning into the quinoa.

Cover and let simmer for 20 minutes. Season with salt and pepper.

Cranberry Salad

Makes 4-6 Servings.

Ingredients

1 cup quinoa, cooked

1 red bell pepper, chopped

1 yellow bell pepper, chopped

1 red onion, finely chopped

1 & ½ tsp curry powder

Chopped cilantro,

The juice from 1 lime

¼ cup sliced or crushed almonds

½ a carrot, grated

½ cup dried cranberries

Salt and black pepper to taste

Directions

In a large mixing bowl add all the ingredients except the salt, pepper and lime juice.

Mix everything well and then season with the remaining ingredients.

Kale and Garlic Salad

Makes 1-2 Servings.

Ingredients

½ cup quinoa, cooked

1 tbsp olive oil

1 cup kale, chopped or shredded

1 red onion, chopped

2 cloves of garlic, minced

Few splashes of sesame oil

2 tbsp water, plus more if needed

Salt and ground black pepper to taste

Directions

Place a pan over a medium heat and add the oil.

Once the oil is heated add the garlic, onion and kale. Cook for 5 minutes stirring frequently.

Season generously with salt and pepper then add the quinoa. Mix everything well.

Add the water to prevent the mixture from sticking to the pan and cook for a further 4-5 minutes.

Take off the heat and splash in the sesame oil. Mix well (add more to taste).

Afrikaans Soup

Makes 4-6 Servings.

Ingredients

2 tbsp unsalted butter

1 onion, finely chopped

1 sweet potato, chopped or cubed

1 red bell pepper, chopped

2 stalks of celery, chopped

2 zucchinis, chopped

1 jalapeno pepper, seeds removed and minced

2 cloves of garlic, minced

6 cups vegetable stock

½ cup quinoa, uncooked

1 tsp ground cumin

1 tsp ground oregano

1 tsp sea salt

Black pepper, to taste

½ tsp ground cayenne pepper

½ cup of smooth peanut butter

Directions

In a large soup pot add the butter and apply a medium heat.

As the butter melts add the garlic, onion, sweet potato, peppers, celery, zucchini and jalapeno. Mix well. Cook for 10-12 minutes or until the vegetables begin to soften.

Add the stock and quinoa. Mix well.

Season with the oregano, cumin, and cayenne. Bring to the boil before adding the salt and pepper.

Reduce the heat to low and cover. Let simmer for 10 minutes before removing the cover and adding the peanut butter. Stir several times to ensure everything is well mixed.

Cover and let simmer for 15-20 minutes.

Hearty Lentil Soup

Makes 4 Servings.

Ingredients

4 cups water

1 cup celery, chopped

1 cup lentils, uncooked

½ cup quinoa, uncooked

½ cup carrot, thinly chopped

½ cup of mushrooms, chopped

1 tbsp ground chilli powder

1 tbsp ground cumin

1 tbsp ground ginger

Directions

Place a soup pot over a medium heat and add the water.

Pour all the other ingredients in and stir well to mix.

Bring to a boil, then lower heat, cover and let simmer for 40 minutes.

Season with salt and pepper.

Sweet Fig Salad

Makes 4 Servings.

Ingredients

1 cup dry sherry

½ cup dried currants

2 cups quinoa, cooked

2 scallions, thinly sliced

1 cup of fresh figs, stem removed and chopped

1 cup of carrot, finely chopped

¼ green bell pepper, chopped

¼ red bell pepper, chopped

¼ cup chopped cilantro

1/3 cup of any citrus vinaigrette

Directions

Place the currants into a small bowl and then cover with the sherry. Set aside and allow them to rehydrate for 15-20 minutes.

Pour the currants into a sieve and set aside whilst sherry drains from them.

In a large mixing bowl add the quinoa and all remaining ingredients (except the vinaigrette). Mix well then add the currants and mix again.

Drizzle the vinaigrette over everything and serve.

Steak and Orange Salad

Makes 3-4 Servings.

Not Suitable for Vegetarian Diet

Ingredients

1 small-medium rump steak

1 cup quinoa, cooked

2 tbsp olive oil

1 broccoli head, chopped into small florets

Handful of sugar snap peas

1 avocado, skin and stone removed, flesh cut into pieces

¼ cup of orange juice

Directions

Place a pan over a medium-high heat and add 1 tbsp of olive oil.

Let the oil get very hot (sizzling point) then add the steak and sear each side for 1 minute.

Once seared turn the heat to medium-low and cook to your liking.

Remove the steak from the pan and set aside. Add the broccoli and peas to the pan, increase to a medium heat.

After 5 minutes of cooking the vegetables add ¼ cup of water and the quinoa. Mix well. Be sure to stir frequently.

Slice the steak into thin strips and return (with its juices) to the pan. Mix well.

As this heats through take a separate bowl and whisk together the remaining olive oil and the orange juice.

Take the pan off the heat when everything is piping hot. Add the avocado and fold in.

Pour the orange juice and oil mix over everything then fold again.

Makes 1 Serving.

Ingredients

¼ cup quinoa, uncooked

3 tbsp olive oil

2 tbsp sunflower seeds

2 cloves of garlic, minced

1 packed cup of spinach

½ a lemon squeezed

¼ cup of cheddar, grated

Directions

Add 2 cups of water to a pot and bring to a boil over a high heat. Add the quinoa and bring back to the boil. Let simmer for about 15-20 minutes before draining and rinsing with cold water.

Set the quinoa aside and place the pan over a medium heat. Add the oil and garlic and cook for 2-3 minutes.

Add the quinoa and spinach to the pan. Mix well.

Once the spinach is wilted add the lemon juice and cheese. Mix well and cook for a further 2-3 minutes.

Hearty Veggie Soup

Makes 6 Servings.

Ingredients

2 tbsp olive oil

1 onion, diced

2 cloves of garlic, minced

2 carrots, finely chopped

2 stalks of celery, chopped

1 zucchini, chopped

1 & ½ cups green beans, cut into pieces

4 cups vegetable broth

1 can diced tomatoes

2 bay leaves

1 tsp dried thyme

1/3 cup basil, chopped

2 cups quinoa, cooked

Salt and black pepper, to taste

Directions

Place a large pot over a medium-low heat and add the olive oil. Once heated add the onion and cook for 5 minutes.

Throw in the garlic and cook for another 2 minutes before adding the celery, zucchini, carrots and green beans. Cook this for 5 minutes stirring frequently.

Pour in the broth and the tomatoes. Mix well.

Add the bay leaves, thyme and basil before reducing the heat to low. Cover and leave cooking for 25 minutes.

Add the quinoa, stir in and season with salt and pepper.

Peanut Butter Protein Bars

Makes 4-8 Servings

Not Suitable for Gluten Free Diet

Ingredients

2 cups quinoa, cooked

2 cups oatmeal

½ cup dried cranberries

½ cup peanut butter, smooth

½ cup milk, skimmed

1/3 cup brown rice syrup

¼ cup ground flaxseed

1 tsp ground cinnamon

Directions

Preheat your oven to 350F.

Grease a baking pan and set aside. The size of the pan will determine the thickness of the bars.

Add all the ingredients to a large mixing bowl and mix well. Use a wooden spoon or your hands.

Spread the mixture onto a baking tray and put in middle shelf of the oven.

Bake for 15-20 minutes.

Remove, let cool, wrap in tin foil and place in refrigerator for 2 hours.

Quinoa Parmesan Bites

Makes 4 Servings

Ingredients

1 & ½ cups quinoa, cooked

2 eggs, beaten

1 onion, thinly sliced

1 clove of garlic, minced

½ cup parmesan cheese, grated

3 tbsp cilantro, chopped

2 tbsp almond flour

Sprinkle of sea salt

Black pepper, to taste

1 tsp fresh lemon juice

1 tsp olive oil

Directions

Preheat your oven to 350F.

Grease a muffin tray (a mini-muffin tray is best) and set aside.

Take a large mixing bowl, add all the ingredients and mix well.

Scoop the mixture into the muffin holes and place in the oven.

Bake for 20-25 minutes.

Sriracha Hot Bites

Makes 4 Servings (around 20 bites)

Ingredients

2 cups quinoa, cooked

¾ cup cheese, grated

2 eggs, beaten

2 green onions, thinly sliced

1 clove of garlic, minced

1 tbsp cilantro, chopped

1 tbsp honey

3 tbsp sriracha

Sprinkle of sea salt

½ cup breadcrumbs

Directions

Preheat your oven to 350F.

Grease a muffin tray (a mini-muffin tray is best) and set aside.

In a large mixing bowl add all the ingredients and mix well. If the mixture isn't sticking together well enough add more breadcrumbs and mix again.

Spoon the mixture into the muffin holes and press firmly down with the back of a spoon or your fingers. Make sure you fill to the top of the hole.

Bake for 18-20 minutes.

Quinoa Chicken & Veg

Makes 4 Servings.

Not Suitable for Vegetarian Diet

Ingredients

1 & ½ cups quinoa, uncooked

2 cups chicken stock

4 tbsp olive oil

2 cloves of garlic chopped

1 onion, finely chopped

2 chicken breasts, cut into strips

1 courgette, chopped

1 tomato, diced

110g feta cheese, crumbled

8 basil leaves

½ a lime, squeezed

Directions

Add the chicken stock to a pot and pour the quinoa on top of it. Stir once and then bring to the boil.

Once boiling reduce the heat to medium-low and cover. Let simmer until the stock is absorbed, usually 15-20 minutes. Fluff with a fork and then set aside.

Add 2 tbsp of the olive oil to a pan and place over a medium heat. Once the oil is heated add the onion and garlic, cook for 5 minutes.

Add the chicken strips and cook for 2 minutes, stirring frequently.

Add the courgette and the tomato. Continue to cook, stirring frequently. Once the chicken is cooked all the way through turn off the heat. Drop in the cheese, basil and lime juice. Mix well.

Serve over hot quinoa.

Pesto Quinoa

Makes 3-4 Servings.

Ingredients

1 & ½ cups quinoa, uncooked

2 cups vegetable stock

3 tbsp basil pesto

2 tomatoes, diced

Sea salt and black pepper to taste

Directions

Add the stock to a large pot and pour the quinoa into it, stir once. Bring to the boil over a medium-high heat.

Reduce the heat to low and let simmer until the stock has been fully absorbed, usually about 15-20 minutes.

Remove from the heat and add the pesto 1 tbsp at a time, stirring before adding the next.

Add the chopped tomato and fold in.

Season generously with salt and pepper.

Chinese Inspired Quinoa

Makes 4 Servings

Ingredients

1 tbsp olive oil

1 & ½ cups quinoa, uncooked

2 cups vegetable stock

3 & ½ tbsp soy sauce

1 tbsp ground ginger

1 clove of garlic, minced

2 spring onions, chopped

Directions

Add the olive oil to a pot and place over a medium heat. Let the oil heat before adding the quinoa and cooking for 2 minutes. Be sure to stir continually to avoid it sticking to the pot.

Add the stock and stir once. Bring to the boil and then lower the heat.

Add the soy sauce, ginger and garlic, stir well. Once everything is mixed cover the pot and simmer for 15-20 minutes. All the stock should have been absorbed by now.

Sprinkle the spring onion over the top before serving.

Makes 4 Servings.

Not Suitable for Vegetarian Diet

Ingredients

3 tsp olive oil

1 onion, chopped

1 cup quinoa, uncooked

1 head of broccoli, chopped

¼ cup raisins

½ cup almonds, chopped or crushed

2 scallions, thinly sliced

4 pieces of cod

1 tsp paprika

Sea salt and black pepper

Directions

Place a pan over a medium heat and add 1 tsp of the oil. Once the oil is heated add the onion and sprinkle with some salt and pepper. Cook for 5 minutes, stirring frequently.

Add the quinoa and 1 & ½ cups of water. Bring to the boil.

Once boiled reduce the heat to low and cover. Let simmer until most of the water has gone, around 12 minutes.

Fold in the broccoli and raisins before covering again. Cook for 10 minutes more (if more water is needed then add it 3 tbsp at a time).

Remove from the heat, fold in the almonds and scallions. Season with salt and pepper. Set aside.

In another pan add the remaining oil and place over a medium-high heat.

Whilst the oil heats up season the cod with paprika, salt and pepper. Add the cod to the pan and cook until opaque. Should be around 4 minutes per side.

Serve with the quinoa.

Sweet Potato, Mushroom and Kale Quinoa

Makes 4 Servings.

Ingredients

1 cup quinoa, uncooked

2 tbsp olive oil

2 small sweet potatoes, peeled and cut into cubes

10 oz. mushrooms, chopped

2 cloves of garlic, minced

1 bunch of kale, torn and with stems removed

¾ cup white wine, a dry white is best

Sea salt and black pepper, to taste

¼ cup of parmesan, grated

Directions

Add 2 cups of water and the quinoa to a pan and bring to the boil.

Reduce the heat to low, then cover and let simmer for 15 minutes, or until all the water is absorbed.

Whilst this is simmering take a large pot and place over a medium heat. Add the oil and heat it. Once the oil is heated add the potatoes and mushrooms. Cook for 5 minutes stirring frequently.

Add the garlic and cook for another 1-2 minutes.

Add the kale, white wine, salt and pepper. Cook for 10 minutes until all the veg is tender. Ensure you are frequently stirring whilst cooking.

When cooked serve this atop the quinoa. Top with grated parmesan.

Stuffed Zucchini

Makes 4 Servings

Ingredients

½ cup quinoa, uncooked

4 zucchinis

1 can cannellini beans

1 cup cherry tomatoes, quartered

½ cup almonds, chopped or crushed

2 cloves of garlic, minced

¾ cup grated Parmesan

4 tbsp olive oil

Directions

Preheat oven to 400F.

In a pan add the quinoa along with 1 cup of water and bring to the boil.

Cover, reduce the heat to medium-low and let simmer until the water is absorbed. Should take 10-15 minutes.

As this simmers cut the zucchinis in half lengthwise. Scoop the seeds and some flesh out. Lay on a baking tray with the cut side facing up.

When the quinoa is cooked add the remaining ingredients and fold in. Season with salt and pepper.

Spoon the mixture into the zucchini halves. Cover with foil and place in the middle of the oven.

Bake for 40 minutes. When the 30 minute mark is up remove the foil and bake uncovered for remaining 10 minutes.

Quinoa Chilli

Makes 3-4 Servings.

Ingredients

2 red bell peppers, chopped

2 red chillies, finely chopped

2 tbsp olive oil

3 cups zucchini, finely chopped

1 & ½ cups onion, finely chopped

4 cloves of garlic, minced

1 tbsp chilli powder

1 tsp cumin

½ tsp paprika

½ cup water

1/3 cup quinoa, uncooked

¼ tsp sea salt

1 can diced tomatoes

1 can kidney beans

1 cup vegetable stock

Directions

Place a large pot over a medium heat and add the olive oil.

Once the oil is heated add the onion, chilli, peppers and garlic. Cook for 3-5 minutes or until the onions begin to turn translucent.

Add the zucchini, chilli powder, cumin and paprika and mix everything together.

Add all the remaining ingredients along with ½ cup of water and bring it to the boil.

Reduce the heat to medium-low when boiling point is reached, then cover and let simmer for 20 minutes.

Makes 4 Servings.

Not Suitable for Vegetarian Diet.

Ingredients

4 golden nugget squashes

1 4" piece of chorizo, chopped

½ cup chopped carrot

1 tbsp olive oil

1 onion, thinly sliced

2 cloves of garlic, minced

½ cup water

2 cups quinoa, cooked

Pinch of chopped parsley

Pinch of chopped thyme

Sea salt and black pepper, to taste

¾ cup of cheese, grated (almost any cheese will work in this recipe)

Directions

Slice the top off of each squash and remove the seeds. Take 4 separate microwave proof bowls or dishes and place 1 squash in each, cut side down. Fill each dish with 1" of water and microwave individually for 10-15 minutes.

Preheat your oven to 350F.

Place a pan over a medium heat and add the olive oil. Once the oil is heated add the garlic, chorizo, onion and carrot to the pan. Cook for 2 minutes, stirring frequently.

Add the water and the quinoa then bring to a boil. Reduce the heat to medium-low, cover and cook for a further 8-10 minutes.

Add half the cheese. Mix everything together and cook for a further 7-10 minutes.

Season with salt and pepper.

Lay your squashes on a baking tray cut side up and stuff each with the quinoa mixture. Sprinkle remaining cheese on top.

Bake for 20 minutes.

Switch the oven to broiler/grill and crisp the tops for 3 minutes.

Makes 4 Servings.

Ingredients

1 & 2/3 cups water

1 cup red quinoa, uncooked (if you can't find red quinoa it doesn't matter)

¼ cup sliced almonds

2 tbsp lemon juice

2 tsp olive oil

3 tsp dark sesame oil

Sea salt, to taste

3 green onions, thinly sliced

Directions

Add the water and quinoa to a pot. Bring to the boil over a medium-high heat.

Once boiled, turn the heat to medium-low, cover and simmer until the water is absorbed. Usually takes between 10-20 minutes.

Whilst this is simmering take a pan and place over a medium heat. Add 1 tsp of the olive oil and heat. When the oil is heated add the almonds and fry them in the oil.

Fry for 2 minutes, stirring continually before adding 1 tsp of the sesame oil and mixing.

Switch off the heat and set aside until the quinoa is ready.

When the quinoa is ready add all the ingredients, along with the almonds, and mix well.

Season with pepper.

Quesadillas

Makes 4 Servings.

Not Suitable for Gluten Free Diet.

Ingredients

¼ cup quinoa, cooked

¾ cup broccoli, chopped

1 cup cheddar cheese, grated

½ cup diced tomatoes from a can

Sea salt and black pepper, to taste

Hot sauce, to taste, optional

2 tsp olive oil

4 medium whole wheat tortillas

Directions

Preheat your oven to 300F.

Take a large bowl and mix together the quinoa, tomatoes, broccoli and cheese. If using hot sauce add it just now as well.

Lay out your tortillas and spoon the mixture onto half of the tortilla then fold the remaining half over the filling. Repeat 4x.

Add 1 tsp of oil to a pan and place over a medium-high heat.

Once the oil is heated add the quesadillas to the pan, if you can only cook one per pan that is fine but ideally do two at a time.

Cook for 2 minutes before carefully flipping and cooking the other side for 2 minutes.

Transfer to a baking tray and keep warm in the oven. Repeat.

Quinoa Cakes with Black Beans & Sweet Potato

Makes 16 cakes, 4 servings.

Ingredients

2 sweet potatoes

6 oz. canned black beans

½ cup quinoa, uncooked

¼ cup gluten free breadcrumbs

¼ cup Parmesan, grated

2 cloves of garlic, minced

¼ cup walnuts, crushed

½ tsp rosemary

½ tsp ground cumin

Sea salt and black pepper, to taste

2 tbsp butter

¼ cup milk

1/3 cup of sour cream

1 tbsp Dijon mustard

Non-stick cooking spray

Directions

Preheat oven to 380F.

Spray 2 baking trays with the cooking spray and set aside.

Use a fork to pierce each potato multiple times. Place on a plate and microwave for 5 minutes. Pierce again a few times and microwave for another 5 minutes. Repeat until they are soft.

Let them cool before removing the skin and cutting the potato into chunks.

Add the potato, butter, cumin, salt and pepper to a large mixing bowl. Mash together.

Add 1 cup of water to a pot and bring to the boil. When boiled add the quinoa and reduce to a low heat. Let the quinoa simmer for 15-20 minutes. The water should be fully absorbed.

Add the black beans and quinoa to the mixing bowl with the potato in it. Fold everything together before adding the cheese, garlic, walnuts, breadcrumbs and rosemary. Mix this all together.

Form this mixture into cake patties and place on the baking trays.

Bake for 15 minutes before flipping and baking the other side for 15 minutes.

Whilst the cakes are baking mix together the mustard and sour cream. Serve this on the cakes when they are finished cooking.

Quinoa Cakes in a Dill and Lemon Sauce

Makes 4-6 Servings

Ingredients

1 tbsp olive oil

½ onion, finely chopped

2 cloves of garlic, minced

2 pressed cups spinach, torn

2 eggs, beaten

1 & ¼ cups cooked quinoa

2 oz. feta cheese, crumbled

1 tbsp chopped fresh dill

¼ tsp lemon zest, grated

Black pepper, to taste

½ cup gluten free bread crumbs

For the Sauce

½ cup plain Greek yogurt

2 tbsp scallions, finely chopped

2 tsp lemon juice

2 tsp fresh dill, chopped

Sea salt and black pepper, to taste

Directions

Preheat your broiler/grill.

Add olive oil to a large pan and place over a medium heat.

Add the onion and garlic, cook for 5 minutes or until the onions are translucent.

Throw the spinach in and cook until it wilts. Ensure everything is well mixed.

Transfer this to a mixing bowl. Add the eggs, quinoa, feta, dill, zest, pepper and bread crumbs to the bowl. Mix well. Leave to stand for 5 minutes.

Grease a baking tray and start making patties to place on it. Make the patties at whatever size you like.

Cook under the broiler for 3-4 minutes before flipping and cooking the other side. Depending on the thickness of your patties you may need to cook for longer.

Whilst they are cooking make the dill and lemon dressing by adding the ingredients to a bowl and mixing well with a fork.

Quinoa Burger Patties

Makes 4-6 Servings.

Directions

3 cups quinoa, cooked

2 cups water

4 cloves of garlic

1 pressed cup spinach

1/3 cup broccoli, chopped

1 red bell pepper, chopped

2 eggs

1 cup of gluten free breadcrumbs

½ cup cheddar, grated

2 tbsp mixed herbs

3 tbsp olive oil

Directions

Place the broccoli and spinach in a microwave proof bowl, add 1" of water and microwave for 3 minutes. After 3 minutes check if the veg has cooked – if not put it back in for 2 minutes.

Add the garlic, pepper, broccoli and spinach to a food processor and pulse until thoroughly chopped.

In a large bowl beat the two eggs before adding the veg mixture. Next add the breadcrumbs and the herbs. Season with salt and pepper before mixing everything together.

Form the mixture into patties and set on a plate. Make as many patties as you can and then place in the refrigerator for 1 hour.

Remove from the refrigerator 15 minutes before cooking to allow them to cool to room temperature.

Take a large pan, place it over a medium-high heat and add the olive oil.

When the oil is heated add the patties and cook for 5-6 minutes per side.

Chicken Balti

Makes 4 Servings

Not Suitable for Vegetarian Diet

Ingredients

1 tbsp olive oil

2 onions, roughly sliced

4 chicken breasts, cut into strips

4 tbsp balti curry paste

1 & ½ cups quinoa, uncooked

1 can chopped tomatoes

3 & ½ cups chicken stock, add more if required

¼ cup salted cashews

Bunch of coriander leaves, chopped

Directions

In a large pan add the oil and place over a medium heat. Once the oil is heated add the onions and cook for 2 minutes.

Add the chicken and brown each side for 3 minutes.

Stir in the paste and quinoa. Ensure everything is well mixed and then cook for 3 minutes.

Add the tomato and the stock. Mix well and let cook for 20-25 minutes.

Take off the heat then add the cashews, the coriander and season with salt and pepper. Mix well.

Makes 3-4 Servings.

Ingredients

2 cups quinoa, cooked

1 tsp olive oil

½ onion, finely chopped

2 tbsp tarragon, chopped roughly

1 can cooked puy or green lentils

¼ cucumber, peeled and diced

⅓ cup feta cheese, crumbled

6 spring onions, thinly sliced

Juice and zest from 1 orange

2 tbsp red wine

Directions

Place a large pan over a medium heat and add the oil. Heat the oil and then add the onion, cook for 5 minutes.

Add the tarragon and stir well for 30 seconds.

Pour in the quinoa and lentils to the pan, mix well. Turn off the heat.

Add the cucumber, feta, springs onions, juice, zest and the red wine vinegar. Fold everything together.

Set aside for 5 minutes to cool. Serve cold.

Simple Stir Fry

Makes 4 Servings.

Ingredients

2 cups quinoa, cooked

5 tbsp olive oil

2 cloves of garlic, minced

3 carrots, thinly sliced into sticks

1 leeks, thinly sliced

1 head of broccoli, chopped into small florets

⅓ cup sundried tomatoes, chopped

2 tsp tomato purée

⅓ cup of stock

Juice from 1 lemon

Sea salt and black pepper, to taste

Directions

Place a large pan over a medium-high heat and add the oil.

Once the oil is heated add the garlic and fry for 1 minute, ensuring you keep it moving.

Add the carrots, leeks and broccoli. Cook for 3 minutes.

Pour in the stock, the quinoa and the tomato puree. Mix well and reduce the heat.

Let the stock be fully absorbed before adding the tomatoes and folding in.

Remove from the heat and garnish with lemon juice, salt and pepper.

Stuffed Tomatoes

Makes 4 Servings.

Ingredients

4 medium tomatoes

Sea salt and black pepper, to taste

1 cup water

½ cup quinoa, uncooked

2 tsp olive oil

3 cups spinach, pressed

2 cloves of garlic, minced

½ tsp chopped fresh parsley

Parmesan cheese, grated, use as much or little as you like

Mozzarella cheese, torn, use as much or little as you like

Directions

Preheat your oven to 375F.

In a pot add the water and quinoa, bring to a boil. Once boiled reduce the heat, cover and let simmer for 15-20 minutes.

Whilst the quinoa cooks cut off the top of the tomatoes and scoop out the flesh inside. Cut a small piece from the bottom of the tomato off (helps it sit flat).

Place a pan over a medium heat and add the olive oil. Once the oil is heated add the garlic and cook for 1 minute.

Throw in the spinach and parsley, cook until wilted stirring frequently. Season with salt and pepper.

Add the quinoa to this pan and mix everything together. Take off the heat.

Spoon the mixture into the hollowed out tomatoes. Cover with foil and bake for 15-20 minutes.

Remove the foil and sprinkle with cheese. Place back in the oven for 5 minutes.

Other Books by Sarah

Baking Gluten Free Bread: Simple Recipes for Busy Moms

Gluten Free Italian: Simple and Delicious Recipes for Cooking Italian Cuisine

The Hot Sauce Book: Recipes for Making Your Own Hot Sauces and Cooking With Them

Green Smoothie Delight: Delicious Smoothie and Juice Recipes to Burn Fat, Improve Your Health and Feel Awesome

Made in the USA
Lexington, KY
07 June 2017